April/Abril

By/Por Robyn Brode

Reading Consultant/Consultora de lectura: Linda Cornwell,
Literacy Connections Consulting/consultora de lectoescritura

WEEKLY READER®
PUBLISHING

Please visit our web site at **www.garethstevens.com**.
For a free catalog describing our list of high-quality books, call 1-800-542-2595 (USA)
or 1-800-387-3178 (Canada). Our fax: 1-877-542-2596

Library of Congress Cataloging-in-Publication Data
Brode, Robyn.
    [April. Spanish & English]
    April / by Robyn Brode ; reading consultant, Linda Cornwell = Abril / por Robyn Brode ;
consultora de lectura, Linda Cornwell.
       p. cm. — (Months of the year = Meses del año)
    Includes bibliographical references and index.
    ISBN-10: 1-4339-1932-X   ISBN-13: 978-1-4339-1932-9 (lib. bdg.)
    ISBN-10: 1-4339-2109-X   ISBN-13: 978-1-4339-2109-4 (softcover)
    1. April (Month)—Juvenile literature.   2. Holidays—United States—Juvenile literature.
    3. Spring—United States—Juvenile literature. I. Cornwell, Linda. II. Title. III. Title: Abril.
    GT4803.A7613   2010
    394.262—dc22   2009013362

This edition first published in 2010 by
Weekly Reader® Books
An Imprint of Gareth Stevens Publishing
1 Reader's Digest Road
Pleasantville, NY 10570-7000 USA

Executive Managing Editor: Lisa M. Herrington
Senior Editors: Barbara Bakowski, Jennifer Magid-Schiller
Designer: Jennifer Ryder-Talbot
Translators: Tatiana Acosta and Guillermo Gutiérrez

Photo Credits: Cover, back cover, title © Masterfile; pp. 7, 9, 21 © Ariel Skelley/Weekly Reader;
p. 11 © Robert Glusic/Getty Images; p. 13 © Sonya Etchison/Shutterstock; p. 15 © Tanya Constantine/
Getty Images; p. 17 © Bobbi Lane/Weekly Reader; p. 19 (top) © Lars Christensen/Shutterstock; p. 19
(bottom) © Carly Rose Hennigan/Shutterstock

Printed in the United States of America

1 2 3 4 5 6 7 8 9 10 11 10 09

Table of Contents/Contenido

Boldface words appear in the glossary.
Las palabras en **negrita** aparecen en el glosario.

Welcome to April!

April is the fourth month of the year.

April has 30 days.

- - - - - - - - - -

¡Bienvenidos a abril!

Abril es el cuarto mes del año.

Abril tiene 30 días.

Months of the Year/Meses del año

Month/Mes	Number of Days/ Días en el mes
1 January/Enero	31
2 February/Febrero	28 or 29*/28 ó 29*
3 March/Marzo	31
4 April/Abril	**30**
5 May/Mayo	31
6 June/Junio	30
7 July/Julio	31
8 August/Agosto	31
9 September/Septiembre	30
10 October/Octubre	31
11 November/Noviembre	30
12 December/Diciembre	31

*February has an extra day every fourth year./Febrero tiene un día extra cada cuatro años.

Spring Weather

April is a **spring** month. In some places, April is known for its spring showers.

- - - - - - - - - -

Tiempo de primavera

Abril es uno de los meses de **primavera**. En algunos lugares, abril es famoso por las lluvias.

April days can also be warm and sunny. In some places, grass starts to grow. Flowers begin to **bloom**.

– – – – – – – – – –

En abril, también puede haber días soleados y cálidos. En algunos lugares, la hierba empieza a salir y las plantas comienzan a **florecer**.

In April, cherry trees bloom in some places. Cherry blossom **festivals** take place when the trees are in bloom.

- - - - - - - - - -

Hay sitios donde los cerezos florecen en abril. Cuando esto sucede, se celebran **festivales** de los cerezos en flor.

**Cherry blossoms in Washington, D.C./
Cerezos en flor en Washington, D.C.**

11

Special Days

April 1 is **April Fools' Day**. Some people play jokes or say silly things. Then they say, "April fool!"

— — — — — — — —

Días especiales

El 1 de abril es el **día de _April Fools_**. Algunos gastan bromas o dicen cosas disparatadas. Después dicen: "_¡April fool!_".

What is your favorite April Fools' Day joke or trick?

— — — — — — —

¿Cuál es la broma que más te gusta gastar el día de _April Fools_?

April 22 is **Earth Day**. On this day, people all over the world help the planet.

— — — — — — — — — —

El 22 de abril es el **Día de la Tierra**. Ese día, gente de todas partes del mundo hace algo bueno por nuestro planeta.

 What are some ways you can help Earth?

— — — — — — — —

¿Qué cosas buenas puedes hacer por nuestro planeta?

The last Friday in April is **Arbor Day**. On this day, people plant trees.

– – – – – – – – – –

El último viernes de abril es el **Día del Árbol**. Ese día, muchas personas plantan árboles.

In some years, the Easter and Passover holidays are in April. People may celebrate Easter by coloring eggs. Some people eat a special meal on Passover.

— — — — — — — — — —

Hay años en que las celebraciones de la Pascua cristiana y la Pascua judía, o Passover, caen en abril. Para celebrar la Pascua cristiana es costumbre pintar huevos. En la Pascua judía, algunos organizan una comida especial.

Easter eggs/
Huevos de Pascua

Passover plate/Platillo
de la Pascua judía

When April ends, it is time for May to begin.

— — — — — — — — — —

Cuando abril termina, empieza mayo.

Glossary/Glosario

April Fools' Day: April 1, a day to play jokes

Arbor Day: a special day when people plant trees

bloom: to blossom, or grow flowers

Earth Day: April 22, a special day when people find ways to help protect Earth

festivals: celebrations

spring: the season between winter and summer, when the air warms and plants begin to grow

- - - - - - - - -

Día de *April Fools*: 1 de abril, día en que se gastan bromas

Día del Árbol: día especial en que se plantan árboles

Día de la Tierra: el 22 de abril, día especial en que se hacen cosas para proteger nuestro planeta

festivales: celebraciones

florecer: salir las flores

primavera: la estación del año entre el invierno y el verano. En primavera, el aire se hace más caliente y las flores y las plantas empiezan a crecer.

For More Information/Más información

Books/Libros

Splish! Splash! A Book About Rain/¡Splish! ¡Splash! Un libro sobre la lluvia. Josepha Sherman (Picture Window Books, 2008)

Spring/Primavera. Seasons of the Year/Las estaciones del año (series). JoAnn Early Macken (Gareth Stevens Publishing, 2006)

Web Sites/Páginas web

Arbor Day Foundation/Fundación del Día del Árbol
www.arborday.org/kids
Read about the history of Arbor Day. Find ideas for ways to celebrate./Conozcan la historia del Día del Árbol y encuentren ideas para celebrarlo.

Earth Day/Día de la Tierra
www.earthday.gov/kids.htm
Find links to fun Earth Day games and activities./Encuentren enlaces con divertidos juegos y actividades para celebrar el Día de la Tierra.

Index/Índice

About the Author

Robyn Brode has been a teacher, a writer, and an editor in the book publishing field for many years. She earned a bachelor's degree in English literature from the University of California, Berkeley.

Información sobre la autora

Robyn Brode ha sido maestra, escritora y editora de libros durante muchos años. Obtuvo su licenciatura en literatura inglesa en la Universidad de California, Berkeley.